Pebbles of Inspiration

Pebbles of Inspiration

By
Daniela Svampa Cowie

YOUCAXTON PUBLICATIONS
OXFORD & SHREWSBURY

ISBN 978-1-913425-47-0
Published by YouCaxton Publications 2020
YCBN: 01

YouCaxton Publications
www.youcaxton.co.uk

*I hope the quotes within this book
warm your hearts and lighten up your days.*

*May they serve you and reach you with all
the love I am sending them with.*

*With love and gratitude,
Daniela Svampa Cowie*

*Every door is an opportunity
waiting to be explored.*

*The road you 'see' in your
mind's eye is the road you
will walk in your reality.
For that... DREAM BIG!*

Tomorrow is a blank page,
just waiting to be filled...
Be yourself and live the story
of your own unique life.
Be proud, be confident and
most of all, be happy.

Whatever your destination
remember to live and enjoy
every single step.

The tranquility lies within you.
You can choose to express it or
shine away from it.
The choice always rests with you.

When you feel life is
weighing you down and
answers escape you, sit and
wait for the mist to clear
because clear it will.

Deep within the soul,
where all secrets rest,
peace reign as all is well.

Smile, as when you do,
the world is that little
bit richer.

*It is not the experience that differs.
It is the individual view that each one
of us holds of that experience.*

*When you are right in the
midst of it and the target still
looks far away, keep your
faith and focus on taking one
step at the time.*

Open your mind, Look further
and beyond...
All that you thought was not...
IS POSSIBLE.

Believe...
You possess all the tools you
need to live a good life.
Unleash the beast!

*Even the roads that are
arduous and twisted can
be walked with ease if you
focus on each step and keep
a sunny disposition.*

*Follow your own path and not
that of others. As only when
you are true to yourself you
will find true happiness.*

Too often we live our lives
fearing to let go,
yet it is often when we do
that our world comes alive.

You are the light...
The colours in your world.

Whenever life presents you with options, always remember to listen to your inner self.
There is where the best answers lie... waiting to be called upon.

Us too like the pebbles on a sea shore, having travelled our own unique journey, will come to lull in our intended place.

*Indulge yourself, give
yourself permission to
receive the wondrous gifts
that life presents you with.*

*With every step we take, with
congruency, courage and belief, we
steadily remove each and every cloud
to unveil the purity of our soul.*

Sail away, into the unknown...
Immersed in the wonderful
mystery that is your life journey.

When a spark ignites the
depth of your essence,
you come face to face
with your truth.

Whether we ascend or descend,
We shape who we become.

You are only prisoner to your limitations
and self-imposed boundaries.
Free yourself... open the door
to an unbounded life.

*Looking closely within, often solicits new
discoveries and uninvited emotions.
It is by embracing and apportioning these
new findings that allow us to move ahead
with clarity and conviction.*

*Disregard all unpleasantness,
opt instead to see all the beauty
that life has to offer.*

There is a place within us
where strength and calm
come together.
Look within and recharge...
the power that is you.

Each step we take helps to form
a piece of the spine of our life...
Choose wisely. Let your essence,
your higher-self guide you.

Recognise your fears, as with this recognition, will come the realisation that, despite them, you can still go on.

If you look hard enough you will see that is often you, who is holding on to those very chains you believed were holing you back.

*Sometimes we just have to step
aside, and stop asking questions.
Let our deepest self reveal to us
our true desires.*

*Your thoughts are immensely
powerful and effective... Take time
to listen to your mind's chatter
because it is this very chatter, that
will sculpt your future.*

*Let the positivity shine that
little bit brighter.
Don't allow fears or worries
to cloud your dreams.*

*Always strive to reflect
into the world the most
truthful part of yourself.*

*Be especially kind to yourself;
you are the longest relationship
you will have in this life.*

*Wake your senses. Let your
light gracefully grow and
dazzle the world.*

*While life ushers you on and takes you
to new places, the memories hold on to
where you have been...
Find the fine line that connects the two
and live in the balance.*

*Don't be afraid of tears,
they wash away the dirt
from the windows of your
soul, allowing light in to
illuminate your path.*

*Live life as if everything is a miracle.
Learn to smile even through the
difficult times.*

*Always remember to
come back home...
HOME TO YOU.*

Learn to be ok with asking for help... It's ok to reach out. We are all here to support each other. You are not alone. We are never alone.

Today see yourself through the eyes of someone that loves you and truly appreciate how special you are.

*Take a wonder into your
fascinating mind and discover
the spectacular powers
that you hold.*

*Don't wait for others to take
the first step...
If YOU feel something, express
it. If YOU want something,
make it happen.*

*When you are called upon,
teach them how to fly. Be the
wind beneath their wings.*

*As a small drop will cause a
ripple, so will a small action
stir your world.*

Often reaching for our dreams,
means trusting every bit
of ourselves and charging
through our fears.

During those times when you lose
your spark, ask yourself: – "What do I
need to do to bring my smile back?"
Then act on your answer, get your
mojo back.

*It is hard to see dreams in
a cluttered mind.
Make sure that what you'd
like to attract is on show.*

*Blossom, as if you were the
most beautiful flower.
Open yourself to life...
Be alive!*

*Begin every day with the
spirit of entering a brand new
exciting adventure; expecting
miracles along the way.*

*May peace, love and
happiness live in you,
today and always.*

*It is often our perception that
makes all the difference...
The shadows and fears that
darkness brings, disappear when
light shines upon them.*

*Each day you write a
section in the book that is
your life story.
Let each chapter
burst with vitality,
joy, excitement and
satisfaction.*

*Let your inner
beauty blossom so
that your life may
reflect your truth.*

*Live each day with the
belief that you can achieve
anything you want.*

*And when you find yourself lay
awake at night...
let your mind wander in your
wonderful imagination.*

*In life we juggle so
many balls and wear
so many hats.
The real trick is to
remain grounded and
true to ourselves.*

Take good care of the spark within your soul. It is no one's responsibility but your own to keep its light alive.

Make it your mission to always include laughter in your day.

You are the author of your own
life, you have the power to make
it a success story. So... aim high,
smile, believe, love, and give
thanks every day for all you
already have.

Love life and life will
love you back.

And as you enter the stillness, let yourself be comforted by the peace and calmness that silence brings.

Don't sit back and watch life pass you by...
Seize the day!

*Lose yourself in all that life has
to offer, as underneath all the
apparent confusion, all is in
fact, in perfect order.*

*Take time to decide what you think
you want because remember, if
you do not make a decision, it's
the same thing as deciding that
everything shall remain the same.*

Your life belongs to you.
Treat it well.
Be kind to yourself.

It is the small things,
the little deeds that
keep darkness at bay.

When the storm is over It is reassuring to know the stars are still there for us to see.

Don't let the pressure to conform knock the vision out of you.

How people behave is their
choice and responsibility.
Your response to it is yours.
Be mindful, it is the latter that
impacts on your life.

Be too busy living to carry
around needless baggage.

Sometimes all it takes is one intense moment of gratitude to bring about the change you want to create.

Challenge any thought that causes you upset. Learn what it is that it's trying to teach you... and release it... let it go.

Love has its own language.
A language that you cannot
find in a dictionary.

In the midst of noise and
confusion, set aside some
'you' time. Sit back and enjoy
the peace of stillness.

For any negative there is a positive.
Always strive to find those positives and
make your world a happier place.

What would it finally cost you if
you do not let go of that bad habit?
Take one step today to reset the
course to a better outcome.
You deserve to live a happy life.

Find a reason to feel alive.
Let your passion shine through.

Giving thanks is the connection
between where you are now and
your chosen desires.

Never judge yourself
on past choices, you did
the best you could with
the information you
had at the time.

Today is a new day.
Dream a new dream...
Trust in yourself.

When people lead you to believe you are not good enough they are often expressing an opinion of themselves rather than a perception of you. Always believe in you!

Compromise without losing yourself.

*Your body's reaction to your
thoughts is a great indicator of your
feelings and attitude
towards your mind's affairs. Let its
sincere responses guide you.*

*Don't let sorrow confiscate
your happiness.*

Imagine... Put all your troubles in a box, close the box tight, and throw it to the bottom of the sea. Walk freely in your new-found peace.

It is not the being, not even the deed that tires us. It is the trying, the over thinking, and often the need to prove ourselves.

In life we will never know how things would have been if we had made different choices. Nevertheless, as long as we act on our best intentions and trust in the process, happiness will unfold before us.

Make space for the unknown future to fill your life with yet-to-come surprises.

Although making decision can be daunting, when we finally do, the thought process is removed giving us immediate relief from the weight that was pressing on our shoulders.

Today mindfully choose to live your life through happiness. Relax your heart, love, laugh... come alive!

*From any shared event, we all
take away different images,
different memories.*

*Never judge or feel judged by
another's words or actions.
We are simply at a different
point of the path, all growing
at a different pace.*

*Our negative self-talk works on us
until we work on it. Break it down,
understand it, positively re-tune
your mind chatter.*

*It is easy to be lured into believing
that our ego founds our whole nature.
Know, that you are so much more
than that. Know, that you hold a
much greater power.*

*When you walk your spiritual path, your
ego fights to keep its power, it plays
with your mind. Ignore its tricks, and
you will soon discover that the power
will shift from your ego onto your heart.*

*Affirmation: –
I choose to live my life
through happiness and joy.*

*Set out with the right
intention, what happens next
is your experience. Do not
judge, let your life story unfold.*

*Shine like the star
that you are.
Today and every day
illuminate your path.*

The customary things the mind hears all day long are disturbance, commotion, noise and arguments; when all it needs is peacefulness, stillness and tranquility.

Look back at your life and be amazed at how far you have come and grown. What will you be able to do tomorrow that you cannot yet do today?

*Be the leader in your own
mind. Aim to protect your
untainted gifts from your
harmful thoughts.*

*Live your own life.
imperfectly, inelegantly
and even defectively; but
live YOUR OWN life.*

You are your own custodian, and as such, you have the responsibility to make your mind a place of peace, order and respect.

Choose your thoughts wisely they precede your dreams' creation.

The right words and tone of voice carry enormous power in getting desired outcomes; but the right thinking, the right mind set are what make those outcomes done deals.

You can choose how you regard the less fortunate experiences in your life. You can choose to see them as curses or as learning strengthening opportunities.

*Why do you fight so hard
against yourself?
At times, although you try your
very best, not everything turns
out as perfect as you wanted.
Ease off. For those times a
different plan has been laid.*

*Whenever something
happens we always react...
what if this time we just sit
back and observe?*

*In order for us to embrace sincere
relationships we must first be
true to ourselves.*

*Don't be so quick to dismiss
others' disclosures, as by doing
so, you might be reaffirming
deep rooted negative self-beliefs
and feelings of insignificance.*

Sometimes if you look
too closely you miss the
bigger picture.

To really solve your
problems go inside
yourself and release
that part of you that
has chosen to live
through struggle.

Too often we try and hold
the world together to stop
ourselves from falling apart.

Don't fight with life,
be prepared instead to
experience it as the gift
that it is... let the gift
unwrap with grace.

*Today give yourself a gift, release
all judgement toward yourself. See
yourself through the eyes of love.*

*Let all painful experience
come to the forth.
Acknowledge them. Release
them. Free your heart.*

Seeing people not as enemies,
but as allies, will ultimately
remove separation; reducing
judgement, anxiety and the
need to compare and compete.

Don't sell yourself short,
You are a wonderful being.
You deserve the best.

Learn to quiet your inner critic and live an amiable peaceful life.

Be the person who confidently walks through life imparting love, kindness and goodwill.

Be the hero in your own life...
be your inspiration.
Always believe in yourself.

Beat the need to act superior
in order to appease feelings of
inferiority. Know your worth.

There are always signs throughout our lives to show us the way. We just need to pay attention

If you don't like the tune your life is playing, change the frequency.

*Imagine what it would be like
to live without self-doubts,
fears and self-blame...
Embody this blissful feeling.*

*Nobody knows you better
than you; so always trust your
own gut feelings above the
judgement of others.*

*Every day you get to create and
shape a new world for yourself.
Make it amazing...
Let your path be inspiring!*

*Never underestimate the
effect of your positive
words, in your life and
that of others.*

Don't make the mistake of putting off being happy. Love and enjoy the here and now.

If you truly wish it, if you fully believe it, you WILL make it happen.

*Rid yourself of your inner
demons. You have the
blessings in your life to
occupy your mind with.*

*Don't suppress your
emotions they are the
'tell signs' of whether
or not you are aligned
with your true self.*

*Don't give your time to worries
and speculative thoughts. You are
wasting your precious time on
something that might never happen.*

*Having healthy self-love is not
selfishness. It ensures we value
and respect ourselves, our own
wishes as well as those of others.*

Forgive and let go of the drama. It dulls your soul, it takes away your beauty.

The present moment is all we have. How we are in this moment and what we do with it is what matters.

We are all beautifully different.
Treasure your originality.

Enjoy the things that add beauty and
happiness to your every day.
Be sure to live a fulfilling life.

Never depreciate yourself.
Meet any compliment with a
"Thank you" not an excuse.

You don't have to be rich,
beautiful or perfect to deserve
love and respect. Accept
nothing less for yourself.

*If you seriously want
to change your life, be
prepared to also change
what surrounds you.*

*Every time you throw yourself into
the future and fill yourself with
dreaded 'what ifs', reel yourself
back into the now and realise that
right here, right now all is well.*

*Guilty feelings or casting blame
do not change situations. So, take
action if you can and if you can't,
forgive, accept, and move on.*

*Wipe away all expectations of
how your future should be. Trust
instead that, what will unfold,
will meet all your needs for you to
achieve your highest level.*

*Believe you are worth it
and get ready to receive.*

*I am.
Two little words. Such a
powerful statement.*

*Raise yourself above all
gossip and judgements.
Walk your walk with
your head held high.*

*Peel off any labels you
have adhered onto
yourself and discover
your full power. Let
your light shine.*

Your past mistakes have helped you become who you are today. However, those mistakes ARE NOT who YOU are.

What if we stopped asking "what if things don't work out?" and we started believing instead that, one way or another, they always do...

On those occasions when
you feel beaten, ask yourself
which of your wonderful
inner resources you have
not yet used.

Break down your
walls. You are so
much more than your
self-limitations.

Each of us have the power to live and breathe happiness and tranquility. They are our natural inner state of being... Return to source.

Life is but a flash. Smile your best smile.

*Let your soul dance to the music
of your heart.
Aligning all that was,
all that is, and all that will be.*

*Each day practice living
the life you want until that
practice becomes your life.*

*Use love and positivity
as dynamite to bring
down any walls created
out of hurt and fear.*

*The negatives in life are a result of
negative thinking, not the cause
of a cosmic debt that needs to
be repaid. We have the power to
change our direction...
The power of positive thinking.*

*All is accomplished by
taking just one step at
the time. So breath,
focus, smile and begin.*

*When something feels right
it is probably time to act, as
chances are you are in line
with your life purpose.*

Peace is in every step we take
as long as we live in awareness.
Indulge in your dreams but don't
forget to live today.

Learn to see the sun shine
through each rain drop
and watch as your life's
perception is transformed.

*Don't just prepare to
live your life. Ensure
you ACTIVELY live it.*

*Let the wonderful sound of silence
uncover your soul's desires.
Listen.*

The happiness you have in your daily life is determined by the amount of positive thoughts you let shine through.

We came to this planet with a given time before we make our exit.Worrying is purposeless. Live happily. Live fully.

Throughout our lives, throughout our thinking, throughout our choices and actions, we always invest in our tomorrows. The thoughts and the living of today create and shape our future.

Be the messenger of joy, laughter and positivity.

Always find a reason to feel alive.
Today dress yourself of your most
beautiful smile.

Trust yourself, your potential, your
essence, your worth.
No matter how unique, always
find your own way.

*Don't allow past events
to spoil the glamour of
your future visions.*

*Listen with all
your senses; speak
with a benevolent,
enlightened heart.*

*Love with all your
being; freely, deeply
and unconditionally.*

*Don't tear yourself apart.
Build yourself up.*

Trust in yourself.
Make your life happen
the way you choose.

Uphold a positive
and friendly manner
to create more
opportunities and
attract positive
outcomes.

*When the mind is calm
a veil of peace and
tranquility descends
upon our all being,
parading sentiments
and exposing solutions.*

*Be the first to
acknowledge and
celebrate your
successes.*

Clear the album of your life of any images that no longer serve you. Make space for the ones that remind you that you are a special being and you have power beyond any self-limitations.

Don't let tears drown your spirit.

*Often rudeness and disrespect
are a person's way of dealing
with their feelings of discomfort
about the situation.
Don't be too quick to judge.*

*We always do the best we
can with the information
we have at the time
and the lessons we have
learned on our way.*

*You don't have to have bad
eyesight to have clouded vision.
Spring clean your mind, your
heart, your soul.*

*Generously give the
gifts of kindness,
warmth and
friendliness.*

*You have the power to
change your life.
Begin by making one
small change today.*

*Accept your brilliance.
You are powerful
beyond belief.*

*When we change
the pictures and the
sounds in our mind
we reshape our life.*

*Take time each day to play,
laugh, love and dream.*

We wait so long to leave painful situations that we have learnt to attribute that pain to the new experiences, rather than see it for the baggage it actually is.

Be creative with your love giving there are so many ways to show you care.

*Refrain from making
other people's opinion
your own, and live the
life you long to live.*

*When your negative
mind chatter calls...
Hang up.*

The support of right and wrong in our choices is dependent on our life experiences. Don't expect others to take the same steps you would.

Overturn your fears, eradicate your doubts. Let your dreams bloom.

When we take time out from our incessant thinking, we empty ourselves of all stress and anxieties.

Make peace with who you are and where you rest, and you will come to known tranquility.

Setbacks are not the end,
just a test to confirm our
sentiment toward our goal.

Truly affirm the power
within you and miracles
begin to happen.

*When we stop running from fears
and decide to face them instead,
we strip them of all power.
Call fear's bluff.*

*Believe that no obstacle is yet
created to hinder your road to
success... move onwards.*

Choose yourself a thought, a
sentence that truly inspires you
and use it every day.
Let it be something that
comforts you, empowers you
and makes you feel great.

Our subconscious mind
is our faithful custodian;
whatever we ask it will
deliver, good or evil.
Tell it your dreams not your
nightmares.

*At times life throws us a sharp turn.
As creatures of habit we often assume that
this can only be for the worse. What we
often fail to appreciate is that sometimes
we have strayed so far from our path of
purpose that life's only option is to take
that ground from under our feet.*

*When you stop resisting
life and embrace gratitude
instead, you allow blessings
to reach you.*

*The past is the past.
It has imparted the relevant lessons to support
our growth and serve its purpose.Thoughts and
reminiscing are not living; it is just imagination
at play. Life is now, in this moment where
that past has guided us to... with the people we
treasure and the moments we choose to create.*

*Be sure to imagine upon your
mind only the things you want
to see reflected in your world.*

Your life is the result of your state of mind. Whether you want love, happiness, richness or success you have to BELIEVE you DESERVE it and BELIEVE YOU HAVE THE POWER to shape your life.

You cannot expect results if you don't know what you want or if your mind is filled with worries and fears.

Only too often to flatter our ego, we lose ourselves and what we believe in. Be wary of the illusion of happiness that this flattery brings.

Magnify your focus on a single desire at the time... Direct and amplify your energies on just that one thing that you want to manifest.

*Stop your conscious mind from changing
the course of your pure inner desires.
Slam the door on thoughts or doubts that
make you stray from your original path.*

*The loneliness we feel cannot be filled
by outside elements but by becoming
friends with ourselves.*

Learn to listen to your inner self.
What you know 'naturally' is of
much better guidance to you and
your journey than anything you will
come to learn from your outer world.

Although we might at times be
shown the darker side of life, it
is still a fantastic world.

No matter how challenging
and intricate or simple and
undarkened a problem might be,
the tools for all solutions are within
you. Learn to self-rely, look within.

Belief in limitation is the only
power that can keep us from flying.
Release the shackles!

*Remaining still is not an option, life
will always move us onwards.
We can let us be dragged along or we
can choose the where and the how.
We always have a choice.*

*Throw out all that doesn't serve you.
Keep a positive mindset.*

*Our life quickly changes when
we choose to be an example of
positive possibilities instead of
reveling in the wounds of our past.*

*Slow down...
Savour this moment...
this breath...
Just be.*

Break free from the tradition of
accepting a mediocre life.
Realise you are limitless.
Dare to live your dreams.

Your mind loves to
prove you right and will
incessantly look for proofs
to sustain your beliefs.

As the storm passes, let yourself be reborn.
Dare yourself to shine a light, brighter
than you ever have before.

Step away from spiraling
negative thoughts, not only do
they not take you anywhere,
they add to life's confusion.

Keep on top of your moments of insecurity. Deal with life one day at a time without letting thoughts of the future distract you from the good that embrace you right now.

While we are quick to watch and judge other's actions, we neglect to take responsibilities for our own. Attend to your own change.

*Learn to find joy in the learnings
of your living instead of relying on
external assurance and approval and
you will come to know serenity.*

*It can be so easy to run from
ourselves, but all denials soon
catch up. Face yourself.
Learn who you are.*

When we take responsibility for ourselves. There can be no more victims, no more villains, no more blame to be placed... that's when we truly learn our way.

There is no outside manifestation that can satisfy you if you don't have peace within yourself.

Always latch on to something inside you, not outside of you.
Within you is where your strengths lie.

Let go of the need to make others wrong.
It's only their opinion... nothing to do with you.

Bring forth all your wisdom.
Use all the lessons your walk in life has
taught you, to make today and all your
tomorrows, ridiculously wonderful.

Every life is special and unique...
make yours count.

Even the bravest had to face their fears at some point in their lives...
Persevere. Believe. Soldier on.

Today is a brand-new day.
Get rid of any feelings or emotions that prevent you from feeling happy or grateful.

To be cross with others implies that you are not responsible for your living, that it is OTHERS whom have control over YOUR life. Remember, it is you that holds the pen that writes your story.

In life it is never a matter of fault but rather, a matter of choice.

Every time we let ourselves be caught in drama and gossip, we lose a piece of our pure and sincere inner self. A very high price to pay for such common, misleading habits.

Take a deep breath and smile at another beautiful day. You are alive... you are blessed.

Sometimes, shaped by our life's difficulties, we raise barriers and ration our love, fearful of wasting it, thus saving it only for the 'worthy' few. At those times it is necessary to remember that we ARE love... we NEVER run out of love.

Every time we help others find their happiness we take one step closer to our own.

*Recognise your strengths without
seeking approval, Recognize
your weaknesses without
self-persecution,
Aim to be the best you can be by
practicing self-love.*

*It is not always easy to see
the path; but that's okay...
sometimes we just need
to stop and take in the
surroundings.*

*As the sun continues its journey and the world
goes about its business, not all, but too many,
fight battles we know nothing about.
Be gentle.*

*Don't listen to people that tell you
how to fly, when they themselves,
have yet to spread their wings and
refuse to leave the ground.*

*Let any thought you create be sparked
by love, every word you speak be
inspired by goodness, and every action
you take be guided by your higher truth.*

*Failure is just an opportunity
for a new beginning... It is all
a matter of perspective.*

While roaming in a past that can't
be changed we risk losing the gifts
we have here and now.
Think carefully of where you
direct your energies.

Train the negative part of your
mind to seek out the silver lining
and you'll come to find peace.

Your life is an accumulation of pearls of wisdom; use these gems to create a better tomorrow for you and all whose life you touch.

And from today onwards I choose to live life. Now... For real.

Often our fears are also the fears of others. It is through communication that we ease anxieties, gain understanding and restore the balance.

Let love be the light that guides your thoughts, your choices, and your every action.

*Don't trade your integrity for a fistful of
cheap gratifying moments. Your truth is
so much more valuable than that...
YOU are so much more valuable than that.*

*Listen. Truly listen...With an
open mind, an open heart.
With the intention to understand,
to learn, and maybe even to help.*

Spend a little while longer
looking into a loved one's eyes.
Put a little more love in every
text or message you send.
Hold on a little tighter when you
give that hug.
Linger a little longer when
sharing that kiss.
Savour each breath you take...

Dance to the music of life
and remember what a
wonderful soul you are.

*The reciting of easily memorised words often,
from lips spill easily.
Token gestures acted out, to look the part, or
for an easy self-whispered 'I tried'; to impress
others or maybe even to reassure oneself.
All is of very little use if not physically, mentally
or emotionally expressed.
Be real. Be true.*

*We can only work with
what we see and feel
from where we have
come to stand.*

*Love yourself with the same
unconditional love you do your
child, the love of your life, your
best friend, your close ones.*

*When the mood is dark
and life looks glum, remember,
you are the one who can colour
your world... Make it bright!*

You are pure MAGIC The
manual and resources are
within you. Pull out all
you need and make all you
dream of come to life.

Bless yourself with
understanding, warmth,
forgiveness, acceptance,
respect, and undiluted love.

*Let go of yesterday's angsts, all that
was done cannot be undone.
Have mercy on yourself.
Let the next story that your mind
replays, be one of love, lessons
learned and acceptance.*

*Sweet is the moment you
realise what a wonderful
miracle of life you actually are.*

When in life you find yourself in quicksand, strip yourself of all that is weighing you down and give yourself the gift of a new lease of life.

So much time we spend worrying that we let our most precious moments go unnoticed. What are worries if not thieves of our joys.

*Sometimes we are 'called' to
people or situations, not so
much for our progress but to
guide another.
The ebb and flow of life...*

*Let go of angst and that which
keeps you 'stuck'. Appreciate
the lesson and move on to
celebrate a new beginning.*

*There is no place for hate when we
accept that, we all make choices
based on our understanding of our
experiences, while searching for peace,
love and enlightenment.*

*Dream big, for stars are
hidden in your soul.
Believe in you, discover
your purpose. Live life in
your own unique way.*

*Accepting the label of victim, martyr
or unequal won't help you grow or
attract positive outcomes.
It will instead fuel negativity and
taint your true worth. Choose to
develop your strengths.*

*Smile at all the token gestures
and obliging acts; turn your back
and walk away. You are
much more worthy than that.*

*In the name of pride many
relationships are broken.
In the name of love many
relationships are revived.
Different influence...
Different outcome.*

*On your way up to reach
your goals remember to
enjoy each step.
Remember to look at the
view from each step of
your journey.*

*We all at times can feel invisible.
It is not because of others' lack of
attention but because of our own.*

*...and when you least expect it
the answer comes and suddenly
it all makes sense...
The lesson is learnt.*

We label love into so many types...
but, love is love...
At its purest level, it remains the
most powerful essence there is.

If we keep settling for less
along the way, the end result
will be a cheap version of our
original dream.
Know your worth.

*Love yourself with all
your might; as despite of
all your flaws, you are
still a beautiful soul.*

*What is love if not the
acceptance of another
soul's expression.*

*Whenever you feel you have lost your
way reconnect to the power within.
Place a full stop and draw a new plan.*

*Serenity is a state of mind,
wash away the fears, BE...
unconditional love.*

*Sometimes we need to trust our
higher power. With our limited
view, we ourselves, can only see a
speck of our infinite possibilities.*

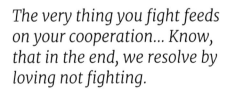

*The very thing you fight feeds
on your cooperation... Know,
that in the end, we resolve by
loving not fighting.*

It takes practice to switch your mind to positive thinking... A worthwhile price for a happier you.

The tears that flood your face today lay the ground for smiles that illuminate your world tomorrow.

Whether you stop or rush,
the lessons meant for you
won't pass you by.
Trust life's rhythm.

No need to fear the new,
everything you have lived
through was new once.

*Let your thirst for life be
bigger than any set back
you may encounter.*

*Focus on your little victories...
Getting out of bed on a 'bad'
day is a victory.*

Smothering someone with time and attention is not love. It is our desperate need to control and feed our own emptiness.

We are so used to putting others on pedestals that we often miss their cry for help.

*No need to escape to get a clean slate.
Learn to make your mind your perfect
living place and you will never need to
run from yourself again.*

*If we look hard enough
we can always find
lessons and blessings in
each occasion in our life.*

Sometimes our need to control is so overwhelming that we forget where our responsibilities end and others begin. Breath... Step back and look again.

Each of us... a bud, with the potential to blossom to a beauty beyond comparison.

Blessings come in many colours but at times we are so fixated on looking for the brighter shades that we fail to recognise the lighter tints.

Nothing in life is ever wasted, everything is a build up to a purpose. We learn, we grow, we live.

Only talk to yourself through the voice of love, kindness and respect, then watch your whole world shine.
Be your number one supporter.

Catapult yourself into a new reality. A reality free of all limitations and abundant with possibilities.

Feeling happiness through outside influences can cause a lot of pain as it is change depending. The power is within... Happiness begins with you.

You are meant to live so much more than an ordinary life; commit to living your extraordinary.

For every in there is an out
For every down there is an up
For every low there is a high.
So when in the dark— Look for the light.
Everything has an opposite...

Sometimes you need to believe in your
uniqueness and take a chance.

The happiness you are looking for is in
every act of kindness you do.
In every smile you give.
In every comforting word you speak.
In every hand you lend.
In every tending of your ear.
Give happiness to find happiness.

There is something inside each and
everyone; a beautiful thing called love...
Let it lead the way.

In spite of any conditioning you have been
subjected to, always keep an open mind.
Life is full of possibilities.

Insecurities and fears are just
thoughts tuned to the wrong
frequency.

The past cannot be undone.
Give your energies and
thoughts to today.
Plant the seeds now for better
happier tomorrows.

Think peaceful
thoughts and your life
will become peaceful.

*In the loneliest hour, look up at
the sky and remember those who
have come to pass before you...
Feel the warmth of their arms
embracing you, their loving
hands supporting you.*

*Keep feeding the fire within,
the passion, the spark that
makes you feel alive.*

*Appreciate where you
have been, be aware of
where you are going,
but always respect the
power of this moment.*

*It does not matter if things don't
turn out the way you expected.
There is always a way out, a new
path to explore.*

Not all is as it first appears...
Let your instinct, not your
emotional state, lead the way.

Embrace the fear of change.
It is this very feeling that will make
your successes taste even sweeter.

...And at that moment, when you realise you could lose it all, you understand the magnitude of your blessings.

Why limit yourself to walk, hop or run...
When you were born to fly!

*No matter where you go, you
can't leave yourself behind.
Take a little time each day to fall
in love with yourself...*

*An open heart is fertile soil for
an open mind. Love opens
all doors. Love is connection.*

You inspire more people than you think. Keep smiling your beautiful smile, keep walking your truth, keep lending your tender hand.

The good you do today will enrich all of your tomorrows.

You can give someone
all the reasons you want
to help them calm their
storm; they will fight you
all the way if they come
from a place of fear and
lack peace in their hearts.

When life gets hard we get to
see the power that we hold.
We are so much stronger than
we realise.

*Reciprocal acceptance begins with
the understanding that we all do
our best in finding our own way.*

*Every time we do an act
of kindness we make this
world a little better.
Keep up the good work.
You are amazing!*

The answers you seek are not in
another's wisdom, in another
country or in another book. The
answers you seek are within you.
Remove the layers.

Like a gardener clears his garden
of unwanted weeds, you must clear
your mind of unwanted thoughts.

Every time you smile you leave a legacy.
Every time you interact you leave a memory.
How can you die and not live an imprint...?
You live—you touch people's lives—you live on...

Always meet another
being with a mind clear of
judgement and expectations.
They are not your past...

*Although you can't
do everything as good
as others do—others
can't do everything as
good as you can do.*

*Our thoughts are the root of
our emotions. The thoughts
we choose shape our mood.*

*Our relationships begin to change when
we see people as they are now rather
then who they have been in the past.*

*Stop pressing the replay button
for memories and feelings
that no longer serve you.*

Don't worry about the times
when you lose who you are,
just keep finding yourself
over and over again.

Feed your mind the
positive side of life.
Begin to focus on the
things you do right.

Make it your aim to only deal with the facts of the here and now instead of those of a hypothetical future.

It is not the occurrence itself that is scary but our thoughts about the occurrence. Try readjusting your perspective...

Whether alone or in the midst of company,
whether resting or busy at work, be fully there.
This moment is all we have.
BE THERE

Savour each breath you take.
Life is now.

A battered mind is an unhappy mind.
Tend to it daily with kind, loving,
grateful thoughts and be amazed as
in return, in its newfound beauty, it
transforms your world.

For all those times you were
let down or 'left behind',
remember... you have been
always there to rescue yourself.

*Our thoughts are at the
root of our emotions.
~Keep them Positive
~Keep them Kind
~Keep them 'Present'
~Keep them Loving
~Keep them Colourful
Keep You Happy*

*No matter what the
situation is, remember to
look for the gem it holds.*

Much can be the root cause of feeling loss; but if we turn to the truth within, we know that in truth, we never lose anyone. There is a beautiful string that joins us all...
At source we are all connected.

Treat yourself to some you time. You too are in need of the attention you so often gift to others.

Life has a knack for catching you by surprise and taking the wind out of you. In those times, battle hard – earn those stripes.
You are stronger than you think...
Remind yourself you are a warrior.

Today affirm...
I am love
I am beauty
I am love
I am happiness
I am life
I am.

*At times we get so drawn in by that
new person, thing or situation that
we neglect essential parts of our life.
Always keep a healthy balance.*

*Your persistence and
bravery will pave the way
and see you 'home'.
Believe in yourself.*

*Even the strongest person cries a
river sometimes; no one is exempt
from the colourful emotions of life.
There is no shame in releasing, it is
liberating to cleanse, to let go.*

*You can't dim a light that is
meant to shine.*

*Too often in a desperate attempt
to 'fix' a painful past we recreate
scenarios that cause additional pain.
Look to heal from the inside.*

*There is always a way out,
a new strategy, a new
path to explore... Nothing is
insurmountable*

When we go through hard times we tend to feel very alone. That is when it's key to remember, we are NEVER alone if we give people a chance. There is always someone willing to help... let them in.

Through the depth of each experience, we learn, we grow, we find life.

Being a friend to someone does not guarantee that they are a friend to you.
Learn to recognise when you are being used or taken for granted and gently walk away.

Take a little time each day to fall in love with yourself...

*Worrying does not change results.
Trust that whatever happens, you
have within you all the 'tools'
required to address and resolve any
situation as it presents itself.*

*No matter how stuck we feel, it
is important to remember that
we are always just a thought
away to turn it all around.*

Love the moment... In this very moment you are experiencing the gift of life; and if you do nothing else but breathe and be present, you'll come to comprehend how special it is.

No matter how adverse the influences, it is still up to us who we choose to become. By taking responsibility we take our power back.

Although we might not understand another person's choice, we must respect that it is their own path they are walking... perhaps the only one they have come to know.

No matter where you are at, be in love with this beautiful gift called life... Each layer we unveil reveals new wisdoms, new beginnings.

*Learn to trust your first feeling,
that raw gut reaction, that
original response. Before you
enter thinking you have your
most truthful answers.*

*In those moments
when darkness takes
over, remind yourself
that you have within
you a sunshine that
can disperse any cloud*

It is often when we are at our lowest that we finally, 'see' ourselves. It is through this identification, as we begin to self-rely, that we learn to fall in love with ourselves.

During times of uncomfortable differences it helps to remember that we all do the best we can in finding our own way.

*Through the role we let our
own mind play in our life we
can create a state of freedom
or prison for ourselves. We are
the ones who choose.*

*Every day is a new opportunity to
create our life the way we want to.
Let us not waste today reminiscing
on yesterday's pain.
Choose peace over drama.*

*Let us focus not on where we
have been but in creating
the happy, more serene, and
fulfilling life, we deserve.
Right here— Right now.
Life is in this moment.*

*Be persistent with a new
habit. Hang in there until it
becomes second nature.
Push past the uncomfortable
stage of change.*

Today is a brand-new day.
Move away from any
thoughts, feelings or emotions
that prevent you from feeling
happy and grateful.

It is often the letting go of
what we have come to believe
that will set us free.
All it takes is one new
thought to open our eyes.

*When we take responsibility for
ourselves there can be no more
victims, no more villains, no
more blame to be placed...
That's when peace can blossom
and we shed our chains.*

*No step is too small when stepping
from the darkness into the light.*

Everything that happens in our life happens in perfect order; for us and those whose lives we touch.

Let the next story that your mind replays be one of love, lessons learned, peace and acceptance.

*It is not easy at times to decipher
what is a true gut reaction and
what is a memory regurgitation of
past deductions. What is important
however, is to remember that even
when we misread and confuse the
two, the power of the next step is
still in our hands.*

*Rise up and shine!
Only you shine this
shade of beautiful.*

*How we talk to ourselves has
a huge impact on our lives.
This talk is the translation
of our experiences; the
difference between
succeeding and giving up...
living and existing.*

*'Doing' and 'Being'...
Both necessary for living
a healthy and balanced life.*

Every day is a new beginning.
Even if for today all you can do is
breathe, breathe purposefully...
breathe in awareness.

Within you...
Around you...
Love is always the answer.

About the Author

Daniela is an integrative therapy counsellor and public speaker. Author of 'A Reason To Love Me', her raw heart-wrenching autobiography and 'A Reason To Love Them – Breaking the chains of trauma', a powerful outlook aimed at taking one's life back. Through her writing Daniela, an avid flag bearer of the message that nothing is insurmountable, aims to bring hope, love and strength to as many people as possible.